T. D. MACDO[N...]
was a writer and po.. .....n a deep interest
in Scots and Gaelic language. As well as
gathering proverbs for this collection,
Thomas Donald MacDonald wrote
The Lords of Lochaber,
Celtic Dialects, Dàin Eadar-
Theangaichte, Dàin an àm Cogaidh
and *Dàin an Dèidh a' Chogaidh.*

Do not pluck
the beard of a stranger

...and other wise Gaelic proverbs

Collected by

T. D. MACDONALD

Selected by

LUATH PRESS

Luath Press Limited

EDINBURGH

www.luath.co.uk

First published 2018
This edition 2023

ISBN: 978-1-80425-115-7

Proverbs sourced – and updated as appropriate to comply
with Gaelic Orthograpic Conventions – from:
Gaelic Proverbs and Proverbial Sayings
by T.D. MacDonald published
by Eneas Mackay, Stirling 1926

The paper used in this book is recyclable. It is made
from low chlorine pulps produced in a low energy,
low emission manner from renewable forests.

Printed and bound by Robertson Printers, Forfar

Design by Tom Bee

Typeset in Mayflower by 3btype.com

CONTENTS

1. MONEY AND WORK

2. FRIENDSHIP AND LOVE

3. NATURE AND WEATHER

4. PERSONALITIES

5. SELF-IMPROVEMENT AND ADVICE

6. CONSOLATION

MONEY
AND
WORK

Uaisle gun chuid, is maragan gun gheir.

Birth without means,
and puddings without suet.

*Those born without money
are at a disadvantage.*

An ràmh as fhaisg' air làimh, iomair leis.

The oar that's nearest,
row with it.

Use what you have.

An rathad fada glan,
is an rathad
goirid salach.

The long clean road,
and the short dirty road.

*If you want something to happen
quickly you might have to cut corners.*

Bidh an t-ubhal as
fheàrr air a'
mheangan as àirde.

The best apple will be
on the highest bough.

*What is the worthiest to achieve
requires the most effort.*

Chan fheum an tì
a shealbhaicheas
an toradh, am
blàth a mhilleadh.

He who would enjoy the fruit
must not spoil the blossom.

*You have to work hard to get
the best outcome.*

Chan uaisle duine na a cheàird.

No man is above his trade.

Nobody is too good to work.

Cha dèanar buannachd gun chall.

There is no profit without loss.

There is no reward without sacrifice.

Am fear nach cuir ri latha fuar, cha bhuain e ri latha teth.

He who will not sow
on a cold day will not reap
on a warm day.

*You have to put in the work
regardless of the circumstances
to reach your goal.*

Am fear a thèid a ghnàth a-mach le lìon, gheibh e eun uaireigin.

He who always sets his net
will get a bird sometime.

*If you are persistent, patient
and prepared you will be rewarded.*

Cha do shoirbhich dithis a-riamh air an aon chnoc.

Two never prospered
on the same hill.

Space is needed to prosper.

Is fheàrr caitheamh na meirgeadh.

Better wear than rust.

Work hard or else decay.

Bheir an èiginn air rudeigin a dhèanamh.

Necessity is the mother of invention.

When you are in need you will find a solution.

Cluinnidh am bodhar fuaim an airgid.

The deaf will hear
the clink of money.

Everyone values money.

Eallach mhòr an duine leisg.

The heavy burden
of the lazy man.

*The lazy will claim
everything is difficult.*

Am fear nach dèan baile air a' bheagan, chan airidh e air a' mhòran.

He who does not work
the small farm is unworthy
of a big one.

*You have to start from the bottom
and work your way up.*

Cha bhi toradh gun saothair.

There will be no produce without labour.

Work to see results.

Cha leasachadh air
droch obair-latha,
a bhith fada gun
tòiseachadh.

A late beginning will not mend
a bad day's work.

*Sleeping in
will not fix a bad day.*

Is fheàrr làn an dùirn
de cheàird na làn an
dùirn a dh'òr.

Better a handful of
craftsmanship
than a handful of gold.

*Money does not make you happy,
work does.*

Is fheàrr sìor-obair na sàr-obair.

Better steady work
than severe spurts of work.

Do not procrastinate.

'S e cleachdadh a nì teòmachd.

Experience makes expertness.

Having experience makes you more knowledgeable in your field.

Am fear a bhios fada gun èirigh, bidh e na leum fad an latha.

He who is late in rising
will be in a hurry all day.

There's no making up for a late start.

FRIENDSHIP
AND
LOVE

An rud a thèid fada
on t-sùil, thèid e fada
on chridhe.

What goes far from the eye
will go far from the heart.

Distance destroys love.

Cha sheas càirdeas air a leth-chois.

Friendship
will not stand on one leg.

*It takes two
to make a friendship function.*

Ceilichidh
seirc aineamh.

Friendship
conceals blemishes.

*A friend's flaws
are easy to ignore.*

Am fear a ghleidheas
a theanga,
gleidhidh e a charaid.

He who holds his tongue
keeps his friend.

*Know when to stay quiet
if you want to keep your friends.*

Is treise dithis
a' dol thar an àtha,
na fad' o chèile.

Two are stronger together,
than far apart
in crossing a ford.

It is easier to overcome problems
together than alone.

Is minig a bha pòsadh
luath na phòsadh
truagh, is am pòsadh
mall na phòsadh dall.

The hurried marriage is often
a tragedy, and the slow to marry
are often blind.

*Be discerning in your choice
of partner, but not so picky
you wait forever.*

Na gabh tè air
bith mar mhnaoi,
a sheallas i fhèin
gun mheang.

Take no woman
for a wife who presents herself
without a flaw.

No one is perfect.

Na chì na bige
's e nì na bige,
na chluinneas iad
's e chanas iad.

What the little ones will see
the little ones will do,
and what they hear
they will repeat.

Children will copy adults.

Tagh do bhean 's a currac-oidhch' oirre.

Choose your wife
with her night-cap on.

*You should see your spouse
at their worst
before you marry them.*

Cha sgeul-rùin e is fios aig triùir air.

It is no secret
when three know it.

*A secret should be kept
between two people.*

Bu mhath an sgàthan sùil caraid.

A friend's eye
is a good looking-glass.

*Friends see you clearly and speak
about you honestly.*

Furain an t-aoigh
a thig, greas an
t-aoigh tha falbh.

Welcome the coming,
speed the parting guest.

*Guests are welcome,
but so is their departure.*

Fàgaidh sìod' is sròl
is sgàrlaid,
gun teine, gun tuar
an fhàrdaich.

Silk and satin, and scarlet,
leave a fireless, colourless hearth.

The material does not make you happy.

Teine chaoran
is gaol giullain,
cha do mhair iad
fada a-riamh.

Peat-fragment fire
and boy's love
never were lasting.

Puppy love never lasts.

Thèid dùthchas an
aghaidh nan creag.

Kinship
will withstand the rocks.

*Family
will outlast hard times.*

An leanabh a
dh'fhàgar dha fhéin,
cuiridh e air a
mhàthair nàire.

The child that's left to himself
will put his mother to shame.

Unwatched children will misbehave.

Comhairle caraid
gun iarraidh,
cha d' fhuair i a-riamh
am meas bu chòir dhi.

A friend's counsel,
unasked, is never esteemed
as it ought to be.

*A friend's unprompted opinion
is not appreciated.*

Cha b' i an t-suirghe
bean gun chostas.

Wooing is a costly dame.

Love is expensive.

Fàinne mun mheòir
's gun snàithne
mun mhàs.

A ring on the finger
and no clothes on the loins.

*A veneer of respectability
sometimes hides bad character.*

Tagh nighean na deagh mhàthar ged a b' e an Diabhal a h-athair.

Choose the good mother's
daughter were the
devil her father.

*Upbringing will affect the child
more than parentage.*

NATURE
AND
WEATHER

'S e 'n èiginn
a chuir an earb
thar an locha.

Necessity made the roe
swim across the loch.

*When you need something
you go to extremes to get it.*

Èirigh tonn
air uisge balbh.

Waves will rise
on silent water.

*A violent storm may occur
when everything
is at its calmest.*

Feumaidh na fithich fhèin a bhith beò.

Even the ravens
must live.

*Every being
has the right to live.*

Tachraidh na daoine,
ach cha thachair
na cnuic.

Men will meet,
but the hills will not.

Friendship is always possible,
in the scheme of things.

Is math an
seirbheiseach teine,
ach 's olc am
maighistir e.

Fire is a good servant,
but a bad master.

*Keep careful control of fire,
it is as dangerous as it is useful.*

Aiteamh na gaoithe
tuatha,
sneachd is reòthadh
anns an uair.

The thaw that comes while
north winds blow will be
followed by frost and snow.

*Do not trust something unexpectedly
good, there might be difficulties ahead.*

Am fear nach cuir
sa Mhàrt,
cha bhuain e san
Fhoghar.

Who doesn't sow in March
will not reap in Autumn.

*You have to do the work
in order to see results.*

An sneachd nach
tig mu Shamhain,
thig e gu reamhar mu
Fheill Brìghde.

The snow that comes not
at Hallowmas, will come thickly
at Candlemas.

*The bad weather
will arrive eventually.*

Breac a' mhuiltein air
an adhar –
bidh latha math
a-màireach ann.

There is a dappled
sky to-day, there will be
a good day to-morrow.

*A cloudy sky one day
means good weather the next.*

Tha an cat san luath,
thig frasan fuara.

The cat is in the ashes,
cold showers are coming.

*A Gaelic superstition
that if a cat sits with its back
to the fireplace, snow is coming.*

Tha an seillean
fo dhìon,
thig gailleann is sian.

The bee has taken shelter,
a storm and rain are coming.

When the bees hide away
the summer is over.

Fàs a' ghrunnd
– a rèir an uachdarain.

The yield of the ground
will depend on the landlord.

*The results of your work
are your responsibility.*

PERSONALITIES

A' bhò as miosa
th' anns a'
bhuaile,
's i as cruaidhe nì
geum.

The worst cow in the
fold lows the loudest.

The worst people are the noisiest.

Beiridh caora dhubh uan geal.

A black ewe
may have a white lamb.

*It is possible to change
for the better.*

Bheir eu-dòchas misneachd don ghealtair.

Desperation
will give courage
to a coward.

In dire times
you will become bold.

Cha tug gaol luath nach tug fuath clis.

Quick to love, quick to hate.

Those who fall in love quickly fall out quickly.

Esan nach fhuiling dochann, chan fhaigh e socair.

He who cannot
suffer pain will not get ease.

*You have to experience
hard times to appreciate
good times.*

Far as
sàmhaiche an
t‑uisge,
's ann as doimhne e.

Still waters run deep.

*A quiet manner
might hide deep passions.*

Far as taine
an abhainn,
's ann as motha a fuaim.

Where the river
is shallowest
it will make the most noise.

The loudest person
might not have the most depth.

Is ladarna gach cù air
a shitig fhèin.

Every dog is bold
on his own midden.

*It is easy to be overconfident
in your own territory.*

Is i an dias as truime,
as ìsle chromas a ceann.

The heaviest ear of corn
bends its head the lowest.

*The genuinely talented
tend to be modest.*

Thèid seòltachd thar spionnadh.

Cunning overcomes strength.

*When you are smart
you do not have to be strong.*

Tha fortan an cuideachd nan treun.

Fortune favours the brave.

*If you are brave
you will create your own luck.*

Labhraidh am
beul, ach 's e
an gnìomh a
dhearbhas.

The mouth will speak,
but deeds are the proof.

*Words are empty,
actions show real intentions.*

Bheir aon fhear each gu uisge ach cha toir a dhà-dheug air òl.

One man can lead a horse to the water, but twelve cannot make it drink.

As hard as you may try, the stubborn cannot be persuaded into action.

Bidh na gobhair bodhar san fhoghar.

The goats will be deaf
at harvest time.

*There's no one as deaf
as those who don't want to hear.*

Cha tig às a' phoit ach an toit a bhios innte.

No fumes from the pot,
but from what it contains.

It is what is at the core that is important, not what is on the outside.

Is bòidhche leis an
fhitheach a
gharraiche-gorm
fhèin.

The raven thinks its own chick
the prettiest.

*You place extra value
on what is your own.*

Rùisgeadh e a thaigh fhèin, a thughadh taigh a choimhearsnaich.

He would bare his own house to thatch his neighbour's.

He would do anything for others.

Am fear a gheibh bàs
gach latha, 's e as
fhaide bhios beò.

He who is dying
every day will live the longest.

Live every day
as if it were your last.

Am fear a bhios
beudach e fhèin,
cha sguir e a
dh'èigneachadh
chàich.

He who is guilty himself
will always be urging others.

The guilty one
always pins the guilt on others.

Am fear a gheibh ainm na mocheirigh, faodaidh e cadal fada.

He who gets the name
of being an early riser may
take a long sleep.

*Work hard and you'll sleep
better at night.*

Am fear
a sheallas roimhe,
cha thuislich e.

He who looks before him
will not stumble.

If you are aware
of what lies ahead,
you will not be caught off guard.

Am fear as clis gu gealladh,
's e as clis gu fealladh.

He who is quickest to promise
is also quickest to deceive.

Those who do not think before
making a promise
are the first to break it.

Aithnichear duine air
a chuideachd.

A man
is known by his company.

*The friends
we choose define us.*

Am fear as ìsle bruidhinn, 's e as fheàrr a chluinneas.

He who speaks the lowest hears the best.

It is easiest to pay attention if you keep quiet.

SELF-IMPROVEMENT
AND
ADVICE

Coin bhadhail
is clann dhaoin' eile!

Stray dogs
and other people's children!

*Other people's children
are often an annoyance.*

Abair ach beagan
is abair gu math e.

Say but little and say it well.

*Say only what you need to say
and choose your words wisely.*

Is fheàrr a bhith
sàmhach na droch
dhàn a ghabhail.

Better be silent
than sing a bad song.

*It is better to keep quiet
than to talk rubbish.*

Cha toir an uaisle goil air a' phoit.

Gentility
will not boil the pot.

*Being passive
will not get you far.*

Feuch gu bheil do
theallach fhèin
sguaibte mus tog thu
luath do
choimhearsnaich.

See that your own hearth is
swept, before you lift your
neighbour's ashes.

*Deal with your own flaws before
pointing out the flaws of others.*

Dèan tàir air do sheana bhrògan nuair a gheibh thu do bhìogain ùra.

Despise your old shoes
when you get your new ones.

Do not live in the past.

Mura comas dhut teumadh, na rùisg do dheudadh.

If you cannot bite,
do not show your teeth.

Do not argue if you've no point.

Is fheàrr a bhith nad aonar na an droch chuideachd.

Better be alone
than in bad company.

*It is better to be alone
than to be surrounded by people
with bad character.*

Na sir 's na seachain an cath.

Neither seek
nor shun the fight.

Do not provoke,
but always stand up for yourself.

An luigh nach fhaighear, chan i a chobhras.

The herb that cannot be found will not give relief.

If it is not working for you, maybe it is not meant to be.

Am fear as fliche, rachadh e don tobar.

He who is wettest,
let him go to the well.

*The one who is the most accustomed
is the one who is the most effective.*

Am fear nach glèidh
na h-airm an àm na
sìthe, cha bhi iad
aige an àm a'
chogaidh.

Who keeps not his arms
in times of peace, will have no
arms in times of war.

If you are not prepared,
you will most likely fail.

Am fear a bhios
fada aig an aiseag,
gheibh e thairis
uaireigin.

He that waits long
at the ferry
will get across sometime.

Be patient.

An nì san tèid dàil, thèid dearmad.

What is delayed
will be forgotten.

*Do not put off things
or they will never happen.*

An rud as fhiach a ghabhail, 's fhiach e iarraidh.

If it is worth taking,
it is worth asking for.

If something is worth it,
pursue it.

Bior nad dhòrn na fàisg;
easbhaidheachd rid
nàmhaid na rùisg;
ri gearradh-sgèine nad
fheòil na èist; bèist
nimheil rid bheò na
dùisg.

A thorn in your grasp, do not squeeze;
thy wants to thine enemy do not bare;
the dagger's point to your flesh do not
hear; a venomous reptile do not rouse.

Do not mess with things that will hurt you.

Beus na tuatha, far am bithear 's e nithear.

The manners
of the folk
where thou art
thou must adopt.

*Adopt the ways of the people
around you.*

Na spìon feusag fir nach aithne dhut.

Do not pluck
the beard of a stranger.

*Do not antagonise
people you do not know.*

Is fheàrr èirigh moch na suidhe anmoch.

Better to rise up early
than to sit up late.

*It is better to start something off early
than to be too late and rush.*

Measar an t-amadan glic ma chumas e a theanga.

The fool may pass for wise
if he holds his tongue.

*If you keep silent
people will not know
you are unwise.*

Is fheàrr a bhith
marbh na bhith nad
thràill reamhar.

Better be dead
than be a fat slave.

*Being free is more important
than being comfortable.*

Buinidh
urram don aois.

Honour belongs to old age.

The elderly deserve respect.

CONSOLATION

An rud nach gabh
leasachadh,
's fheudar cur suas
leis.

What cannot be helped
must be put up with.

*What you cannot help
you have to accept.*

Cha do dhùin doras nach do dh'fhosgail doras.

No door closes
without opening
another door.

There is always hope.

Ged is grinn an sìoda, is coma leis cò air am bi e.

Though the silk be fine,
it cares not who wears it.

*Your appearance
does not define your character.*

Gheibh an t-uaibhreach leagadh, an uair as àirde e.

The proud will get a fall
when at their highest.

*Do not think of yourself too highly
or else you will fail.*

Cha do shèid gaoth
a-riamh nach robh
an seòl chuideigin.

No wind ever blew
that did not fill someone's sails.

Every event is good for someone.

Is tric a bheothaich srad bheag teine mòr.

A small spark
has often kindled a great fire.

*A small action
can trigger a considerable outcome.*

Lìonar beàrn mòr le clachan beaga.

Great gaps
may be filled with
small stones.

*Small steps
will lead you to your goal.*

A' chungaidh-leighis as goirte,'s i as motha tha dèanamh feum.

The medicine that hurts the most is generally the best healer.

The most difficult solution is usually the most effective change to 'medicine'.

Chan i a' mhuc as
sàmhaiche
as lugha a
dh'itheas den
drabh.

It is not the quietest sow
that eats the least.

*Meek is not the worst
thing to be.*

Luath Press Limited

committed to publishing well written books worth reading

LUATH PRESS takes its name from Robert Burns, whose little collie Luath (*Gael.*, swift or nimble) tripped up Jean Armour at a wedding and gave him the chance to speak to the woman who was to be his wife and the abiding love of his life. Burns called one of 'The Twa Dogs' Luath after Cuchullin's hunting dog in Ossian's *Fingal*. Luath Press was established in 1981 in the heart of Burns country, and now resides a few steps up the road from Burns' first lodgings on Edinburgh's Royal Mile. Luath offers you distinctive writing with a hint of unexpected pleasures.

Most bookshops in the UK, the US, Canada, Australia, New Zealand and parts of Europe either carry our books in stock or can order them for you. To order direct from us, please send a £sterling cheque, postal order, international money order or your credit card details (number, address of cardholder and expiry date) to us at the address below. Please add post and packing as follows: UK – £1.00 per delivery address; overseas surface mail – £2.50 per delivery address; overseas airmail – £3.50 for the first book to each delivery address, plus £1.00 for each additional book by airmail to the same address. If your order is a gift, we will happily enclose your card or message at no extra charge.

Luath Press Limited
543/2 Castlehill
The Royal Mile
Edinburgh EH1 2ND
Scotland

Telephone: 0131 225 4326 (24 hours)
email: sales@luath.co.uk
Website: www.luath.co.uk